by Joel Amato
illustrated by Laurie Conley

SCHOOL PUBLISHERS

Printed in China

ISBN 10: 0-15-358404-1
ISBN 13: 978-0-15-358404-6

Ordering Options
ISBN 10: 0-15-358356-8 (Grade K On-Level Collection)
ISBN 13: 978-0-15-358356-8 (Grade K On-Level Collection)
ISBN 10: 0-15-360656-8 (package of 5)
ISBN 13: 978-0-15-360656-4 (package of 5)

4 5 6 7 8 9 10 0940 15 14 13 12 11 10 09

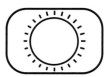

Look at the sun.
Ron can go.

Ron got a cap.

Ron got a kit.

Ron got a bag.

Ron got a rod.

Ron got a gas can.

Ron got it for you, Pam.